Hippocrene
CHILDREN'S
ILLUSTRATED
IRISH
DICTIONARY

ENGLISH - IRISH
IRISH - ENGLISH

Compiled by the Editors of Hippocrene Books

Translation and pronunciation: Seán Ó Briain, translator and interpreter in the Irish Parliament in Dublin.

Interior illustrations by S. Grant (24, 81, 88); J. Gress (page 10, 21, 24, 37, 46, 54, 59, 65, 72, 75, 77);
K. Migliorelli (page 13, 14, 18, 19, 20, 21, 22, 25, 31, 32, 37, 39, 40, 46, 47, 66, 71, 75, 76, 82, 86, 87);
B. Swidzinska (page 9, 11, 12, 13, 14, 16, 23, 27, 28, 30, 32, 33, 35, 37, 38, 41, 42, 45, 46, 47, 48, 49, 50, 52,
53, 56, 57, 58, 59, 60, 61, 62, 63, 66, 68, 69, 70, 71, 72, 73, 75, 77, 78, 79, 83), N. Zhukov (page 8, 13, 14,
17, 18, 23, 27, 29, 33, 34, 39, 40, 41, 52, 64, 65, 71, 72, 73, 78, 84, 86, 88).

Design, prepress, and production: Graafiset International, Inc.

Cataloging-in-Publication Data available from the Library of Congress.

ISBN 0-7818-0713-1

Printed in Hong Kong.

For information, address:
Hippocrene Books, Inc.
171 Madison Avenue
New York, NY 10016

INTRODUCTION

With their absorbent minds, infinite curiosities and excellent memories, children have enormous capacities to master many languages. All they need is exposure and encouragement.

The easiest way to learn a foreign language is to simulate the same natural method by which a child learns English. The natural technique is built on the concept that language is representational of concrete objects and ideas. The use of pictures and words are the natural way for children to begin to acquire a new language.

The concept of this Illustrated Dictionary is to allow children to build vocabulary and initial competency naturally. Looking at the pictorial content of the Dictionary and saying and matching the words in connection to the drawings gives children the opportunity to discover the foreign language and thus, a new way to communicate.

The drawings in the Dictionary are designed to capture children's imaginations and make the learning process interesting and entertaining, as children return to a word and picture repeatedly until they begin to recognize it.

The beautiful images and clear presentation make this dictionary a wonderful tool for unlocking your child's multilingual potential.

Deborah Dumont, M.A., M.Ed.,
Child Psychologist and Educational Consultant

Irish Pronunciation

1. Vowels

In Irish, vowels may be short or long. Long vowels have a long accent shown above them (for example á, é, í, ó, ú).

Letter	Pronunciation system used
a (= short a)	**o** more like the o-sound in English 'bottle' or 'cot.' Sometimes the *a* represents a neutral unstressed vowel, much like the very short unstressed English uh-sound or eh-sound in 'dollar.'
á (= long a)	**aw** as in English 'lawn.'
ao, aoi	**ee** as in English 'sheen.'
e (=short e)	**e** sometimes represents a neutral unstressed vowel, much like a very short English uh-sound or eh-sound like in English 'father.'
é (long e)	**ay** as in English 'hay.'
ea (=short ea)	**a** pronunciation used for a short *e* in combination with *a*, pronounced like *ah* in English 'pal' or 'shall.'
ei (=short ei)	**e** short *e* in combination with *i* is pronounced like *eh* in English 'help.'
i (= short i)	**i** short ih-sound as in English 'tip' or 'lip.' This letter is also found in combination with *a* = *ia*, to give an ee-ah-sound.
í (long i)	**ee** as in English 'sheen.' Sometimes it is followed by an *o* and it is then pronounced like the *ea* in English 'fear.'
o (=short o)	**u** like the uh-sound in English 'luck.'
ó (= long o)	**ow** as in English 'owe.'
u (=short u)	**u** like the short u-sound in English 'book.'
ú (= long u)	**oo** as in English 'mood' or *ew* in English 'crew.'

2. Consonants

Irish has two types of consonants, broad (velar) and slender (palatal). Each written consonant (except *h*) can be broad or slender. Broad consonants are usually preceded or followed by *a*, *o* or *u*, and slender consonants by *i* or *e*. Broad consonants are more like English double consonants, for example *l* is like *ll* as in English 'ball,' *m* like *mm* as in English 'humming,' while slender consonants have a very slight yeh-sound when at the beginning or in the middle of a word, as in English 'mule' or 'canyon,' and a very slight ih-sound before them when at the end of a word. The English examples given below are an approximate guide. Slender consonants are represented with a tick (').

Letter	Pronunciation system used
Broad bh	**v** as in English 'vow'. In the middle of a word, it has a w-sound like in English 'bower.'
Slender bh	**v'** as in English 'veer' but with a more slender quality.
Broad ch	**ch** is a broad, soft guttural ch-sound like in the Scottish pronunciation of 'loch.'

Letter	Pronunciation system used
Slender ch	**ch'** is a slender ch-sound formed by pressing the tongue to the lower front teeth and letting air pass between tongue and palate.
Broad d	**d** pronounced like the English *th* in 'those.'
Broad dh	**gh** a guttural g-sound like the *g* in Spanish 'agua'. Between two vowels the middle of a word, it has a w-sound like in English 'bower.'
Slender dh	**y'** like the *y* in English 'year.'
fh	This letter combination, whenever written in Irish, is silent.
Broad gh	**gh** has the same guttural g-sound as *dh*. Between two vowels in the middle of a word, it is a w-sound like in English 'bower.'
Slender gh	**gh'** like the Spanish *g* in 'agua' but with a slender yeh-quality.
h	**h** is nearly always used after another letter to convey a different sound. When used at the beginning of a word in some borrowings from English, its sound is exactly like the *h* in English 'hat.'
Broad mh	**v** with a broad quality like the *v* in English 'voice.'
Slender mh	**v'** has a slender quality like the *v* in English 'veer.'
Broad ph	**f** like the *f* in English 'father.'
Slender ph	**f'** like the *f* in English 'finger' but with a more pronounced slender quality.
Broad r	**r** like the *r* in English 'rose'. Note that, exceptionally, *r* is always broad at the <u>beginning</u> of a word in Irish, even when followed by *i* or *e*.
Slender r	**r'** has no English equivalent. It is pronounced like the *r* in English 'steer' with the tongue towards the front of the palate.
Slender s	**sh** always pronounced as the English *sh*. No tick necessary.
sh	**h** is pronounced like the English *h* in 'hat.'
Broad t	**t** is a sound half way between the *t* in English 'toe' and *th* in English 'thought.'
Slender t	**t'** is somewhat like the *t* in English 'tin' but with a very slight chi-quality like the *ch* in English 'chin.'
th	**h** as the *h* in English 'hat.'

The letters j, v, w, x, y and z occur only in a small number of loan words where the pronunciation is almost identical to English.

airplane

eitleán
et'-l'awn

alligator

ailigéadar
al'-ig'aydur

alphabet

aibítir
ab'-eet'ir'

antelope

antalóp
ant-alowp

antlers

beanna
b'an-a

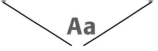

apple   **úll**
ool

aquarium   **uisceadán**
ish-k'adawn

arch   **stua**
stoo-a

arrow   **saighead**
sy-ud

autumn   **fómhar**
fow-vur

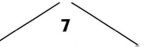

baby **babaí**
bob-ee

backpack **cnapsac**
kunop-sok

badger **broc**
bruk

baker **báicéir**
bawk'-ayr'

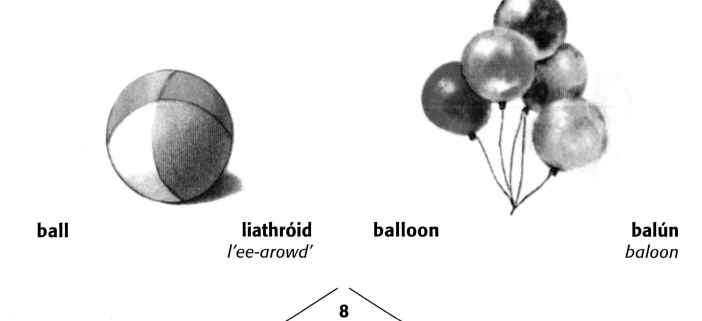

ball **liathróid**
l'ee-arowd'

balloon **balún**
baloon

banana   **banana**
bononn-a

barley   **eorna**
owr-na

barrel   **bairille**
borr-il'i

basket   **bascaed**
bosk-ayd

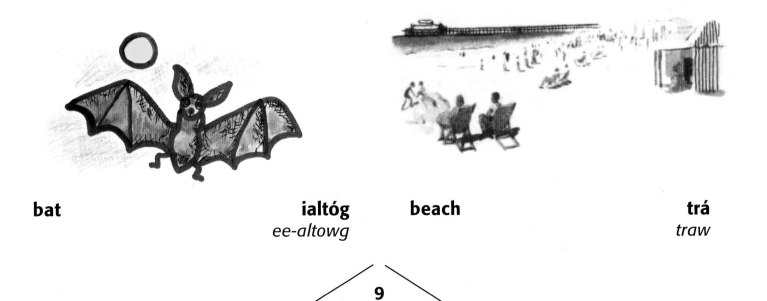

bat   **ialtóg**
ee-altowg

beach   **trá**
traw

bear　　　　　　**béar**
　　　　　　　　　b'ayr

beaver　　　　　**béabhar**
　　　　　　　　　b'ay-vur

bed　　　　　　**leaba**
　　　　　　　　　l'ab-a

bee　　　　　　**beach**
　　　　　　　　　b'ach

beetle　　　　　**ciaróg**
　　　　　　　　　k'ee-arowg

bell　　　　　　**clog**
　　　　　　　　　klug

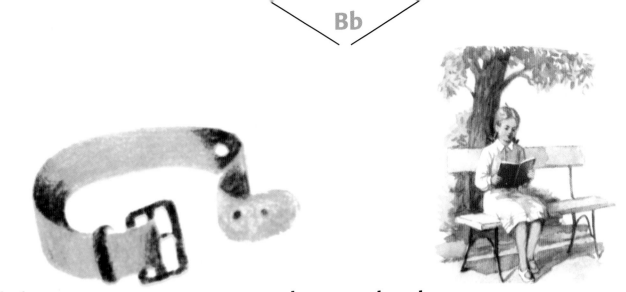

belt   **crios**
kr'iss

bench   **binse**
b'in'-shi

bicycle   **rothar**
ruh-ur

binoculars   **déshúiligh**
d'ay-hool'-ee

bird   **éan**
ayn

birdcage   **éanadán**
ayn-udawn

black   **dubh**
dov

blocks   **bloic**
blok'

blossom   **bláth**
blaw

blue   **gorm**
gur-um

boat   **bád**
bawd

bone   **cnámh**
kunawv

book **leabhar**
l'ow-ur

boot **buatais**
boo-atish

bottle **buidéal**
bwid'-ayl

bowl **babhla**
bow-la

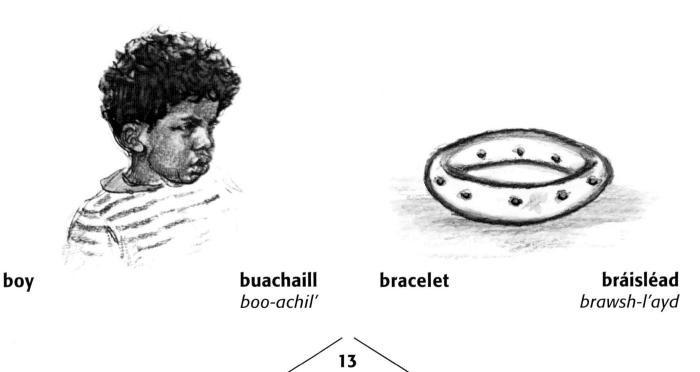

boy **buachaill**
boo-achil'

bracelet **bráisléad**
brawsh-l'ayd

branch   **craobh**
                   kreev

bread   **arán**
                   orrawn

breakfast   **bricfeasta**
                   brik-f'asta

bridge   **droichead**
                   dru-hud

broom   **scuab**
                   skoo-ab

brother   **deartháir**
                   d'ar-hawr'

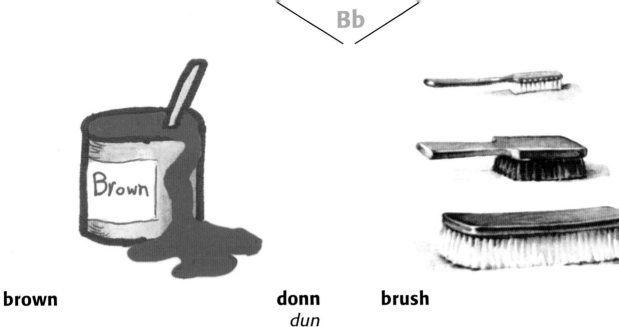

brown   **donn**
dun

brush   **scuab**
skoo-ab

bucket   **buicéad**
bwik'-ayd

bulletin board   **bord faisnéise**
bowrd fosh-n'aysh-i

bumblebee   **bumbóg**
bum-bowg

butterfly   **féileacán**
f'ay-l'ukawn

cab **cab**
kob

cabbage **cabáiste**
kob-awsh-t'i

cactus **cachtas**
koch-tuss

café **caife**
kof'-eh

cake **cáca**
kaw-ka

camel **camall**
komm-ul

camera   **ceamara**
k'am-ura

candle   **coinneal**
kun'-ul

candy   **milseáin**
mill-shawn'

canoe   **naomhóg**
nee-vogue

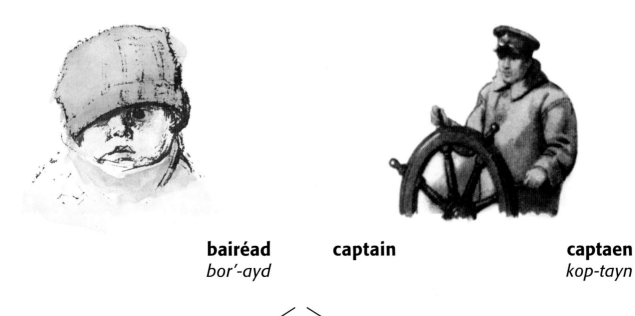

cap   **bairéad**
bor'-ayd

captain   **captaen**
kop-tayn

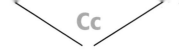

car   **carr**
kawr

card   **cárta**
kawr-ta

carpet   **cairpéad**
kor'-p'ayd

carrot   **cairéad**
kor'-ayd

(to) carry   **iompair**
ump-ir'

castle   **caisleán**
kosh-l'awn

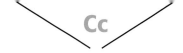

cat   **cat**
kot

cave   **pluais**
ploo-ash

chair   **cathaoir**
koh-eer'

cheese   **cáis**
kawsh

cherry   **silín**
shil'-een'

chimney   **simléar**
shim'-l'ayr

chocolate   **seacláid**
shok-lawd'

Christmas tree   **crann Nollag**
kron null-ug

circus   **sorcas**
sur-kuss

(to) climb   **dreap**
d'r'ap

cloud   **néal**
n'ayl

clown   **áilteoir**
awl'-t'owr'

coach   **cóiste**
kowsh-t'i

coat   **cóta**
kow-ta

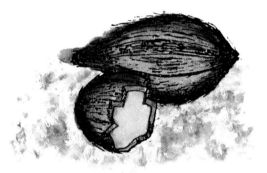

coconut   **cnó cócó**
kunow-kow-kow

comb   **cíor**
k'eer

comforter   **cuilteog leapa**
kwil'-t'owg l'ap-a

compass   **compás**
kum-pawss

(to) cook   **cócaráil**
cow-kurawl'

cork   **corc**
kurk

corn   **arbhar**
orr-avur

cow   **bó**
bow

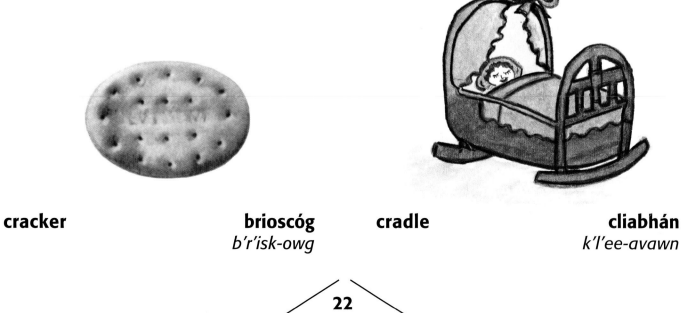

cracker   **brioscóg**
b'r'isk-owg

cradle   **cliabhán**
k'l'ee-avawn

(to) crawl   **lámhacán**
law-vukawn

(to) cross   **trasnaigh**
tras-nee

crown   **coróin**
kur-own'

(to) cry   **caoin**
kween'

cucumber   **cúcamar**
koo-kumar

curtain   **cuirtín**
kwirt'-een'

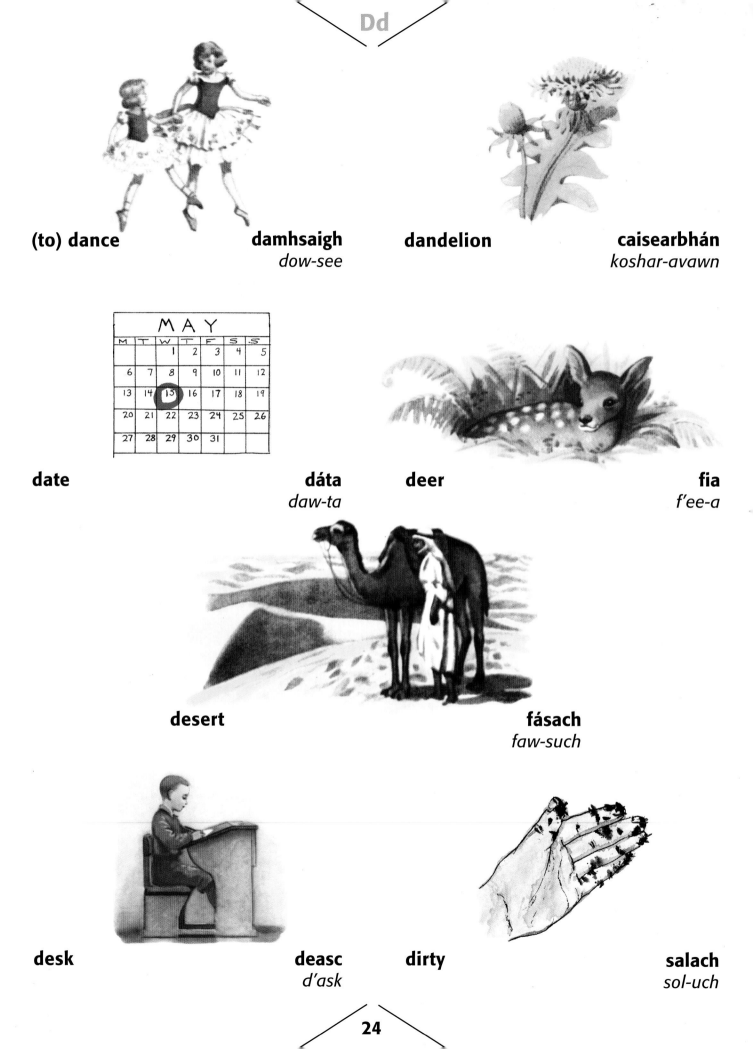

(to) dance   **damhsaigh**
dow-see

dandelion   **caisearbhán**
koshar-avawn

date   **dáta**
daw-ta

deer   **fia**
f'ee-a

desert   **fásach**
faw-such

desk   **deasc**
d'ask

dirty   **salach**
sol-uch

dog

madra
mod-ra

doghouse

cró madra
krow mod-ra

doll

bábóg
baw-bowg

dollhouse

teach bábóg
t'och baw-bowg

dolphin

deilf
d'el'f'

donkey

asal
oss-ul

dragon

dragan
drog-un

dragonfly   **snáthaid mhór**
snaw-hid' vowr

(to) draw   **línigh**
l'ee-n'ee

dress   **gúna**
goo-na

(to) drink   **ól**
owl

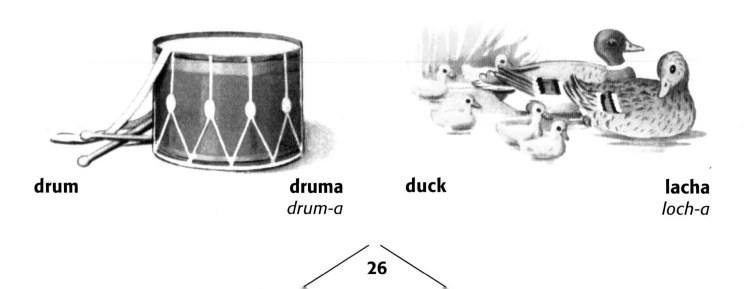

drum   **druma**
drum-a

duck   **lacha**
loch-a

eagle   **iolar**
ull-ur

(to) eat   **ith**
ih

egg   **ubh**
oov

eggplant   **ubhthoradh**
oov-hura

eight   **ocht**
ucht

elbow   **uillinn**
il'-in'

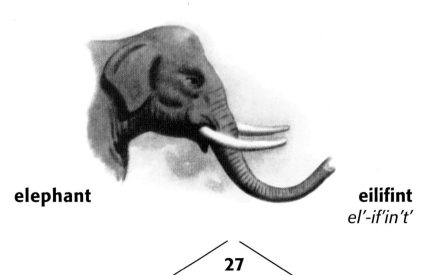

elephant   **eilifint**
el'-if'in't'

empty   **folamh**
foll-uv

engine   **inneall**
in'-ul

envelope   **clúdach litreach**
koo-duch l'it'-r'uch

escalator   **staighre beo**
sty-r'i b'ow

Eskimo   **eiscimeach**
esh-k'im'uch

(to) explore   **taiscéal**
tash-k'ayl

eye   **súil**
sool'

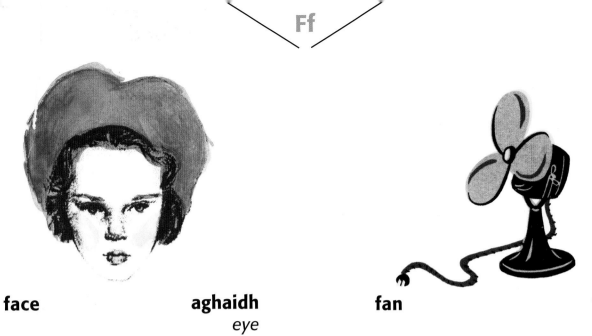

face **aghaidh**
eye

fan **fean**
f'an

father **athair**
a-hir'

fear **eagla**
og-la

feather **cleite**
kl'et'-i

(to) feed **cothaigh**
kuh-hee

fence **fál**
fawl

fern **raithneach**
rah-n'uch

field **páirc**
pawr'k'

field mouse **luch fhéir**
luch-ayr'

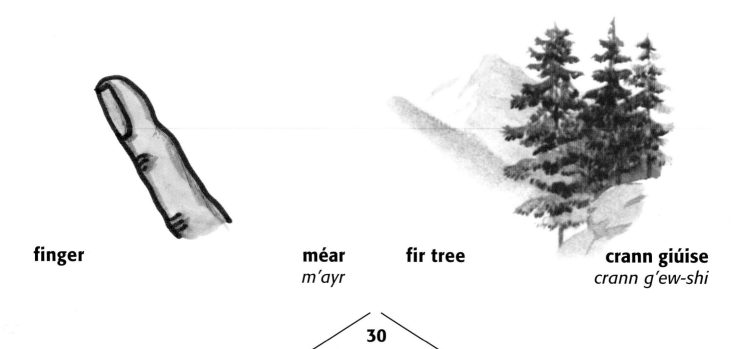

finger **méar**
m'ayr

fir tree **crann giúise**
crann g'ew-shi

fire **tine**
t'in'-i

fish **iasc**
ee-ask

(to) fish **iascach**
ee-askuch

fist **dorn**
dowrn

five **cúig**
koog'

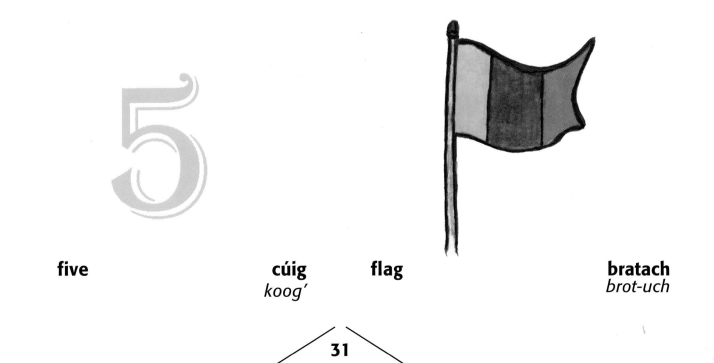

flag **bratach**
brot-uch

flashlight   **splancsolas**
              splonk-sul-us

(to) float   **snámh**
                      snawv

flower   **bláth**
                      blaw

(to) fly   **eitil**
              et'-il'

foot   **cos**
                      kuss

fork   **forc**
        furk

fountain   **fuarán**
                    foo-arawn

four

ceathair
k'ah-ir'

fox

sionnach
shunn-uch

frame

deilbh
d'el'-iv'

friend

cara
kor-a

frog

frog
frug

fruit

toradh
tur-a

furniture

troscán
truss-kawn

garden   **gairdín**
gawr-d'een'

gate   **geata**
g'at-a

(to) gather   **cruinnigh**
krin'-ee

geranium   **geiréiniam**
g'er'ayn'-ee-am

giraffe   **sioráf**
sherawf

girl   **cailín**
kol'-een'

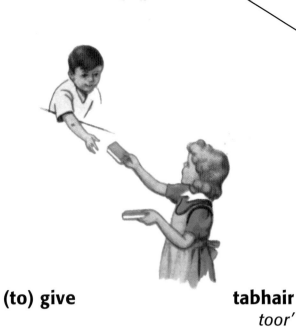

(to) give   **tabhair**
toor'

glass   **gloine**
glun'e

glasses   **spéaclaí**
sp'ay-klee

globe   **cruinneog**
krin'-owg

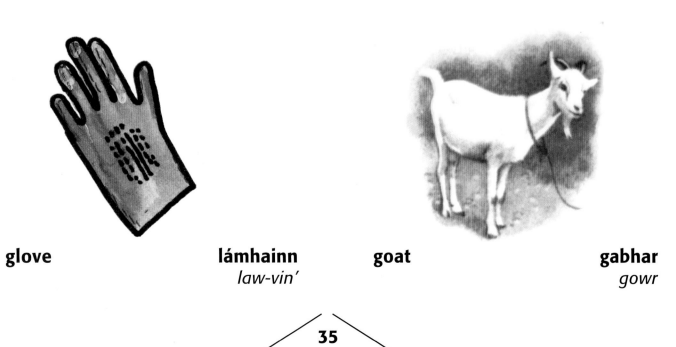

glove   **lámhainn**
law-vin'

goat   **gabhar**
gowr

goldfish

iasc órga
ee-ask owr-ga

"Good Night"

oíche mhaith
ee-hu voh

"Good-bye"

slán
slawn

goose

gé
g'ay

grandfather

seanathair
shan-ah-hir'

grandmother

seanmháthair
shan-vaw-hir'

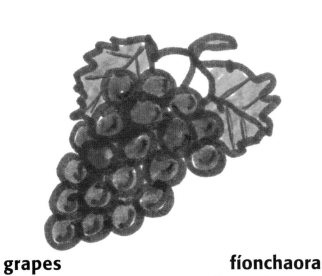

grapes **fíonchaora**
f'een-chweera

grasshopper **dreoilín teaspaigh**
d'r'ow-l'een' t'ass-pee

green **uaine**
oo-an-e

greenhouse **teach gloine**
t'och glun'-e

guitar **giotár**
g'itawr

hammer   **casúr**
koss-oor

hammock   **ámóg**
aw-mowg

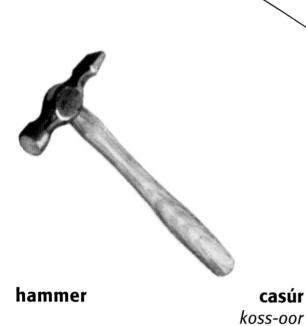

hamster   **hamstar**
hom-stur

hand   **lámh**
lawv

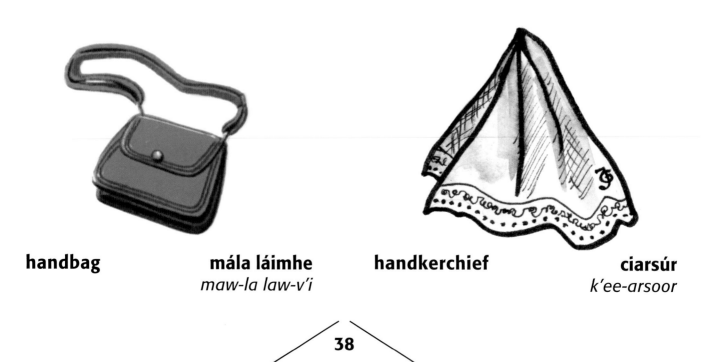

handbag   **mála láimhe**
maw-la law-v'i

handkerchief   **ciarsúr**
k'ee-arsoor

harvest **fómhar**
fow-vur

hat **hata**
hot-a

hay **féar**
f'ayr

headdress **ceannbheart**
k'an-v'art

heart **croí**
kree

hedgehog **gráinneog**
graw-n'owg

hen   **cearc**
k'ark

(to) hide   **ceil**
k'el'

highway   **mórbhealach**
mowr-v'al-uch

honey   **mil**
m'il'

horns   **adharca**
ayr-ka

horse   **capall**
kop-ul

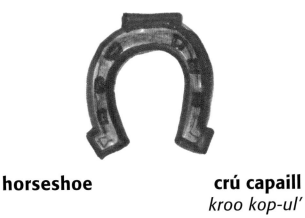

horseshoe **crú capaill**
kroo kop-ul'

hourglass **orláiste**
owr-lawsh-t'i

house **teach**
t'och

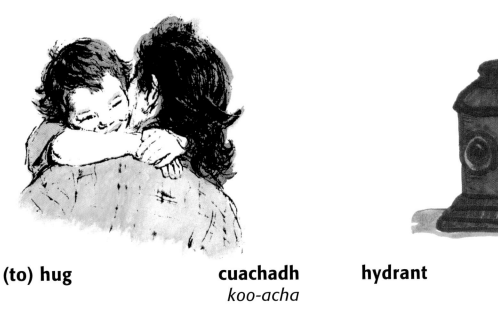

(to) hug **cuachadh**
koo-acha

hydrant **hiodrant**
hid-runt

ice cream　　**uachtar reoite**
oo-achtur rowt'-e

ice cubes　　**ciúbanna oighir**
k'oob-una ayr'

ice-skating　　**oighearscátáil**
ayr-skaw-tawl'

instrument　　**gléas**
gl'ayss

iris　　**feileastram**
f'el'-ustrum

iron　　**iarann**
ee-arun

island　　**oileán**
il'-awn

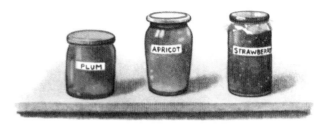

Jj

jacket　　　　　**casóg**
koss-owg

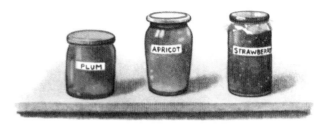

jam　　　　　**subh**
soov

jigsaw puzzle　　**míreanna mearaí**
m'eer'-una m'ar-ee

jockey　　　　　**jacaí**
jok-ee

juggler　　　**lámhchleasaí**
lawv-chlass-ee

(to) jump　　　　　**léim**
l'aym'

kangaroo　　　　**cangarú**
kong-guroo

key　　　　**eochair**
uch-ir'

kitten　　　　**piscín**
p'ish-k'een'

knife　　　　**scian**
shk'ee-an

knight　　　　**ridire**
rid'-ir'e

(to) knit　　　　**cniotáil**
k'en'it'-awl'

knot　　　　**snaidhm**
sny-im

koala bear　　　　**béar cóála**
b'ayr kow-aw-la

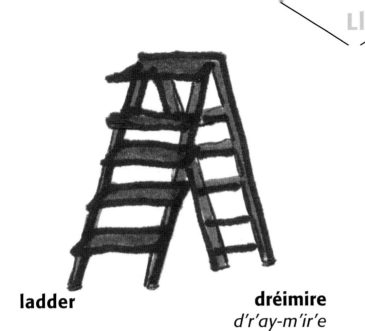

ladder

dréimire
d'r'ay-m'ir'e

ladybug

bóin Dé
bow-een' d'ay

lamb

uan
oo-an

lamp

lampa
lom-pa

(to) lap

ól
owl

laughter

gáire
gaw-r'i

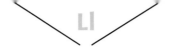

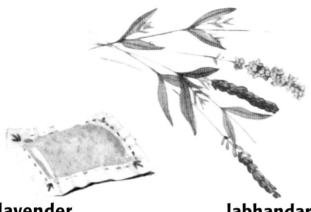

lavender　　　　　　**labhandar**
lov-undar

lawn mower　　　　**lomaire faiche**
lum-ir'e fa-ha

leaf　　　　　　　**duileog**
dil'owg

leg　　　　　　　**cos**
kuss

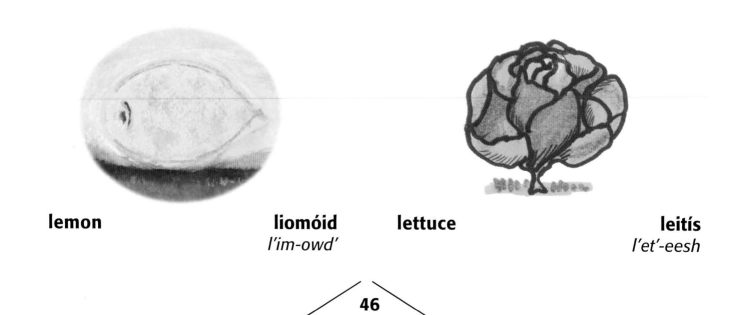

lemon　　　　　**liomóid**
l'im-owd'

lettuce　　　　　**leitís**
l'et'-eesh

lightbulb　　　**bolgán solais**
bul-ugawn sul-ish

lighthouse　　　**teach solais**
t'och sul-ish

lilac　　　**liathchorcra**
l'ee-achurk-ra

lion　　　**leon**
l'own

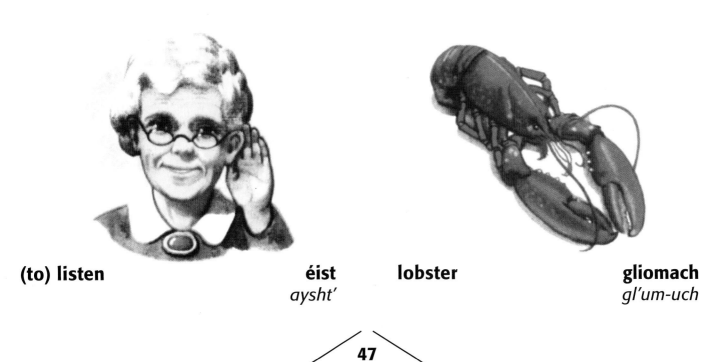

(to) listen　　　**éist**
aysht'

lobster　　　**gliomach**
gl'um-uch

lock   **glas**   **lovebird**   **pearaicít**
gloss   *p'ar-uk' eet'*

luggage   **bagáiste**   **lumberjack**   **lománaí**
bog-awsht'i   *lum-awnee*

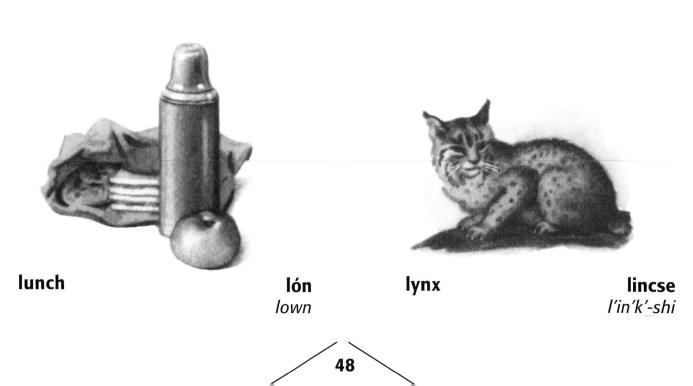

lunch   **lón**   **lynx**   **lincse**
lown   *l'in'k'-shi*

magazine **iris**
ir'r'-ish

magician **draíodóir**
dree-udowr'

magnet **maighnéad**
moy-n'ayd

map **léarscáil**
l'ayr-skawl'

maple leaf **duileog mailpe**
dil'-owg mal'-p'i

marketplace **margadh**
mor-uga

mask **masc**
mosk

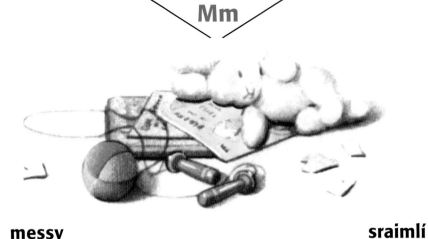

messy

sraimlí
srom'-l'ee

milkman

fear bainne
f'ar bon'-i

mirror

scáthán
skaw-hawn

mitten

dornóg
dowr-nowg

money

airgead
arr-ig'ud

monkey

moncaí
munk-ee

moon

gealach
g'al-uch

mother   **máthair**
maw-hir'

mountain   **sliabh**
shl'ee-av

mouse   **luch(óg)**
luch(owg)

mouth   **béal**
b'ayl

mushroom   **beacán**
b'ak-awn

music   **ceol**
k'owl

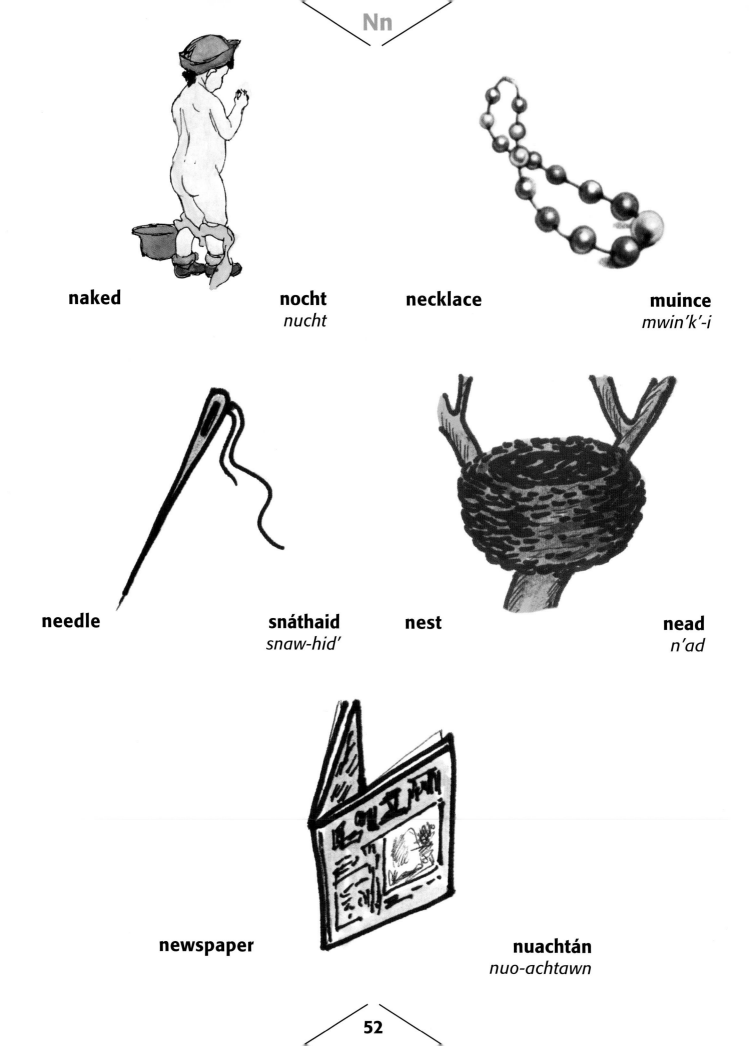

naked   **nocht**
nucht

necklace   **muince**
mwin'k'-i

needle   **snáthaid**
snaw-hid'

nest   **nead**
n'ad

newspaper   **nuachtán**
nuo-achtawn

nightingale **filiméala** **nine** **naoi**
f'il'-im'ay-la *nee*

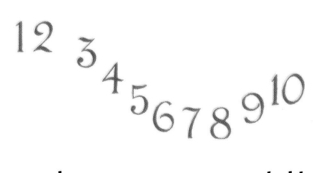

notebook **leabhar nótaí** **number** **uimhir**
l'ow-ur now-tee *iv'-ir'*

nut **cnó**
kunow

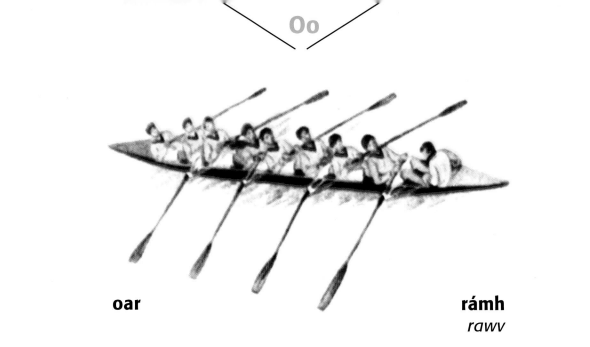

oar **rámh**
rawv

ocean liner **linéar aigéin**
l'een'-air ag'ayn'

old **aosta**
eesta

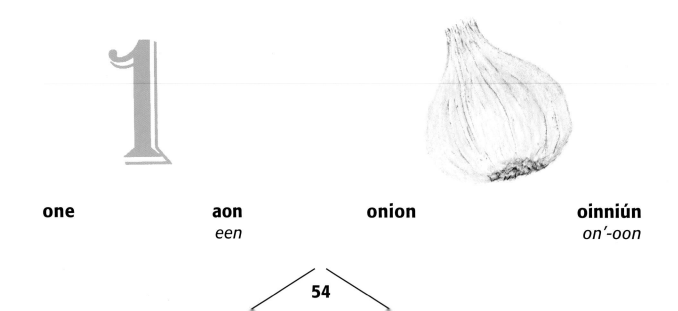

one **aon** **onion** **oinniún**
een *on'-oon*

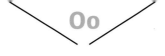

open   **ar oscailt**
er uss-kilt'

orange   **oráiste**
urr-awsht'i

ostrich   **ostrais**
uss-trish

owl   **ulchabhán**
ool-chuvawn

ox   **damh**
dov

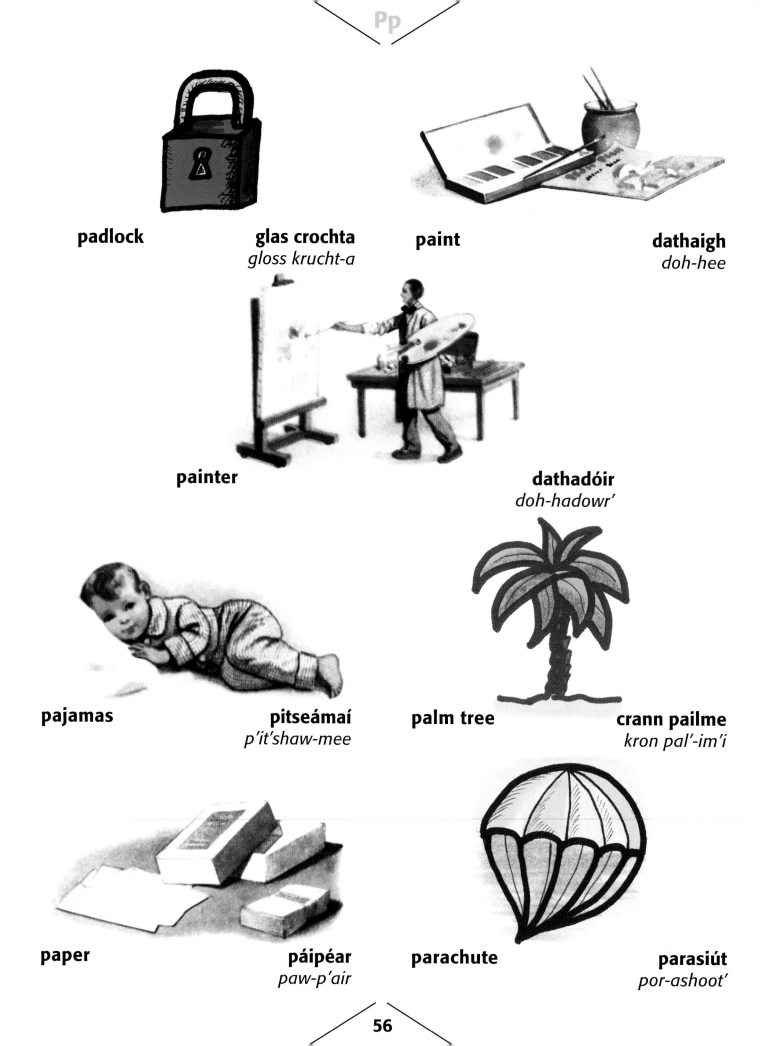

padlock   **glas crochta**
gloss krucht-a

paint   **dathaigh**
doh-hee

painter   **dathadóir**
doh-hadowr'

pajamas   **pitseámaí**
p'it'shaw-mee

palm tree   **crann pailme**
kron pal'-im'i

paper   **páipéar**
paw-p'air

parachute   **parasiút**
por-ashoot'

park

páirc
pawr'k'

parrot

pearóid
p'ar-owd'

passport

pas
poss

patch

paiste
posh-t'i

path

cabhsa
kow-sa

peach

péitseog
p'ayt'-showg

pear

piorra
p'irr-a

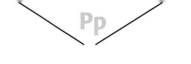

pebble

púróg
poor-owg

(to) peck

pioc
p'uk

(to) peel

scamh
skov

pelican

peileacán
p'el'-ukawn

pencil

peann luaidhe
p'an loo-ee

penguin

piongain
p'ing-un'

people

pobal
pub-ul

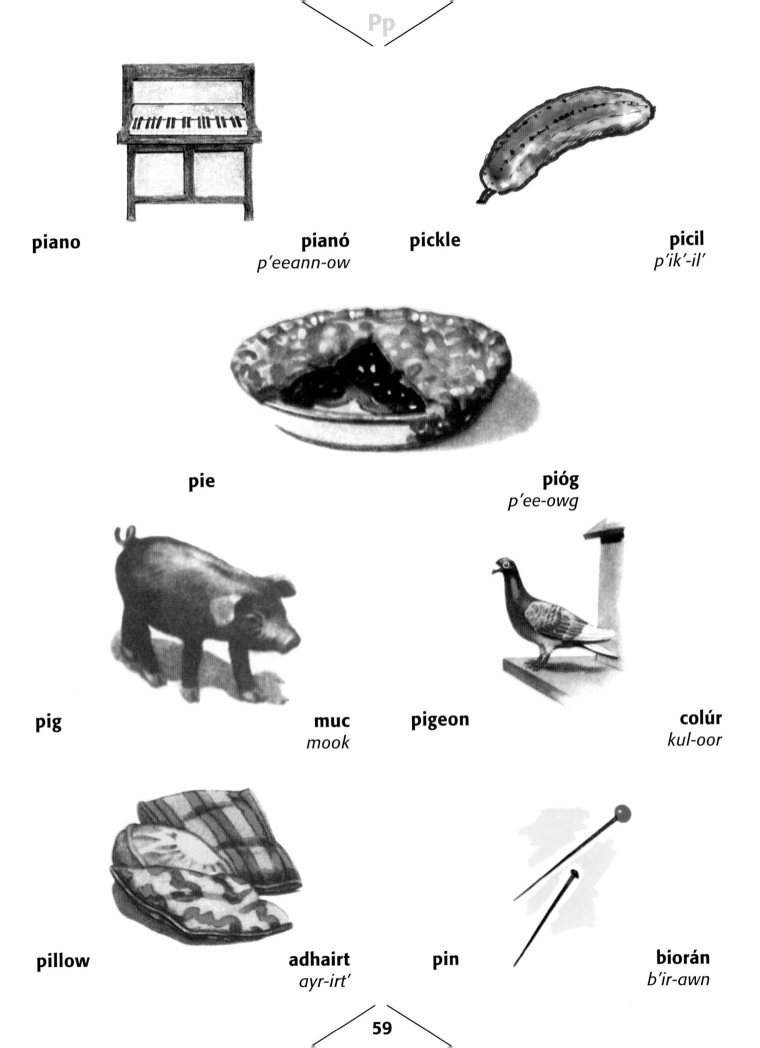

piano

pianó
p'eeann-ow

pickle

picil
p'ik'-il'

pie

pióg
p'ee-owg

pig

muc
mook

pigeon

colúr
kul-oor

pillow

adhairt
ayr-irt'

pin

biorán
b'ir-awn

pine **crann péine**
kron p'ay-n'i

pineapple **anann**
on-un

pit **logall**
lug-ull

pitcher **crúsca**
kroos-ka

plate **pláta**
plaw-ta

platypus **platapas**
plot-upus

(to) play **déanamh spraoi**
d'aynuv spree

plum **pluma**
plum-a

polar bear **béar bán**
b'ayr bawn

pony **pónaí**
pow-nee

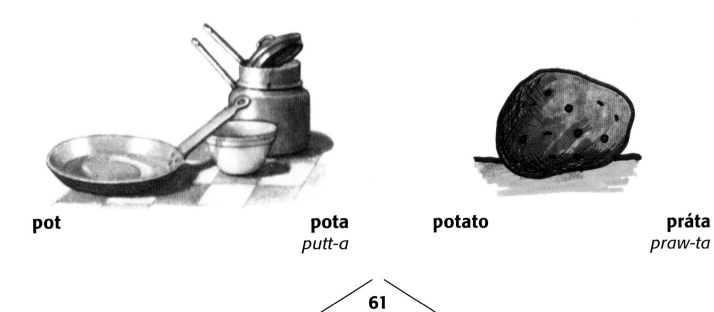

pot **pota**
putt-a

potato **práta**
praw-ta

(to) pour　　　　　　**doirt**
durt'

present　　　　　　**bronntanas**
brun-tunus

(to) pull　　　　　　**tarraing**
torr-in'g'

pumpkin　　　　　　**puimcín**
pwim'-k'een'

Qq

puppy　　　　　　**coileán**
kul'-awn

queen　　　　　　**banríon**
bon-reen

rabbit

coinín
kun'-een'

raccoon

racún
rok-oon

racket

raicéad
rak'-ayd

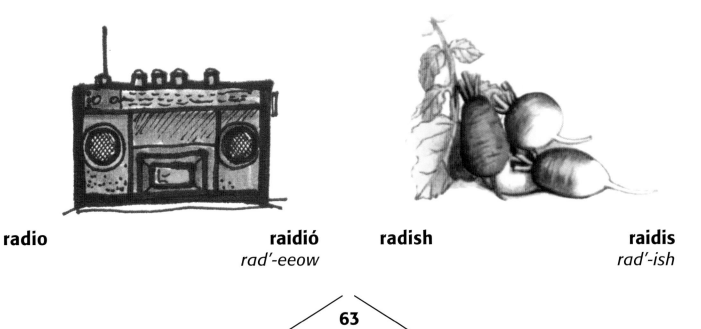

radio

raidió
rad'-eeow

radish

raidis
rad'-ish

raft **rafta** **rain** **báisteach**
rof-ta *bawsh-t'uch*

rainbow **tuar ceatha**
too-ar k'ah-a

raincoat **cóta báistí** **raspberry** **sú craobh**
kow-ta bawsh-t'ee *soo kreev*

(to) read **léigh**
l'ay

red **dearg**
d'ar-ug

refrigerator **cuisneoir**
kwish-n'owr'

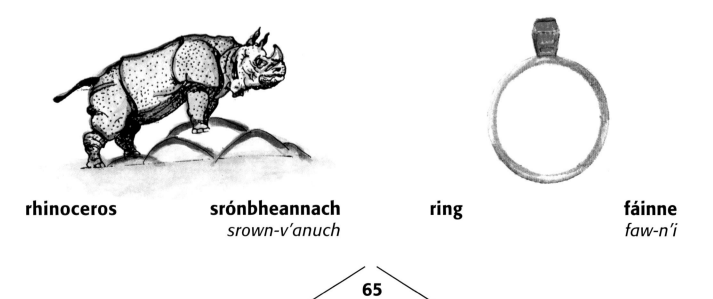

rhinoceros **srónbheannach**
srown-v'anuch

ring **fáinne**
faw-n'i

(to) ring   **cling**
k'l'in'g'

river   **abhainn**
aw-in'

road   **bóthar**
bow-hur

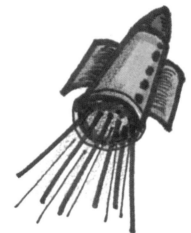

rocket   **roicéad**
rok'ayd

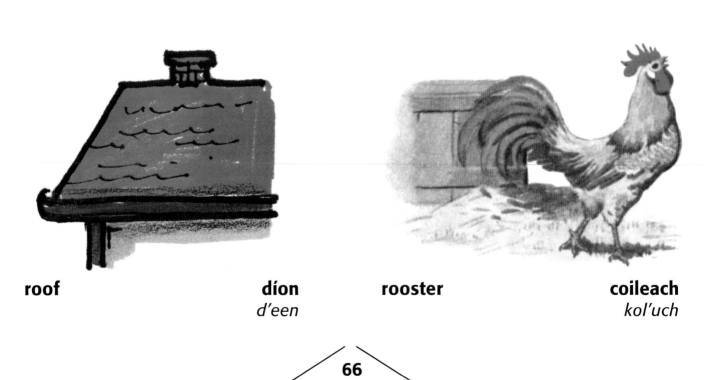

roof   **díon**
d'een

rooster   **coileach**
kol'uch

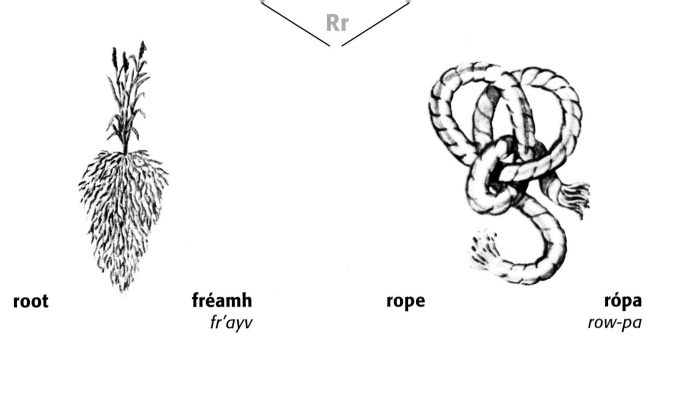

root **fréamh** *fr'ayv*	**rope** **rópa** *row-pa*

rose **rós** *rowss*	**(to) row** **rámhaigh** *raw-vee*

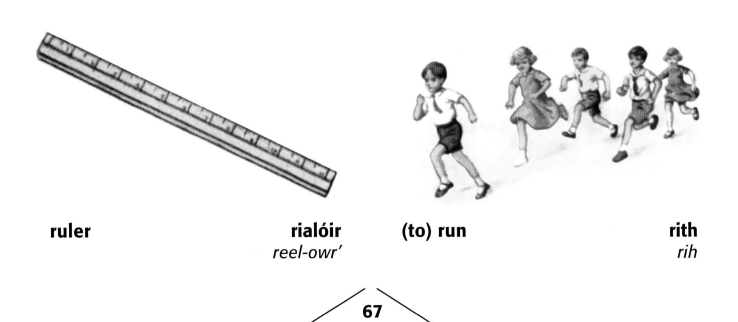

ruler **rialóir** *reel-owr'*	**(to) run** **rith** *rih*

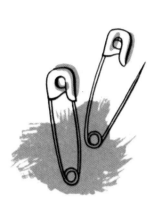

safety pin   **biorán sábháilteachta**
b'ir-awn sawvawl'-t'uchta

(to) sail   **seol**
showl

sailor   **mairnéalach**
mawr-n'ayluch

salt   **salann**
sol-un

scarf   **scaif**
skaf'

school   **scoil**
skul'

scissors **siosúr**
shiss-oor

screwdriver **scriúire**
s'k'r'oo-ir'i

seagull **faoileán**
feel'-awn

seesaw **maide corrach**
mod'i kur-uch

seven **seacht**
shocht

(to) sew **fuaigh**
foo-ee

shark　　　　**siorc**
skurk

sheep　　　　**caora**
keera

shell　　　　**sliogán**
shl'ig-awn

shepherd　　　　**aoire**
eer'-a

ship　　　　**long**
lung

shirt　　　　**léine**
l'ay-n'i

shoe   **bróg**
browg

shovel   **sluasaid**
sloo-asud'

(to) show   **taispéain**
tash-p'awn'

shower   **cith**
k'ih

shutter   **comhla**
kow-la

sick   **tinn**
t'in'

sieve   **criathar**   **(to) sing**   **can**
k'r'ee-ahur   *kon*

(to) sit   **suigh**   **six**   **sé**
see   *shay*

sled   **carr sleamhnáin**   **(to) sleep**   **codail**
kawr shlow-nawn'   *kud'-ul'*

small   **beag**
b'eg

smile   **aoibh**
eev'

snail   **silide**
shel'-id'i

snake   **nathair**
nah-hir'

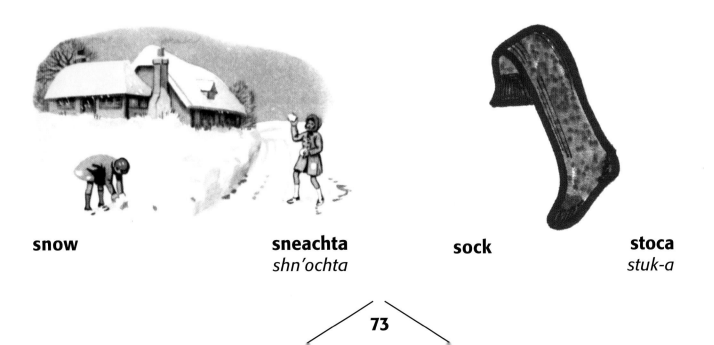

snow   **sneachta**
shn'ochta

sock   **stoca**
stuk-a

sofa   **tolg**
tul-ug

sparrow   **gealbhan**
g'al-avon

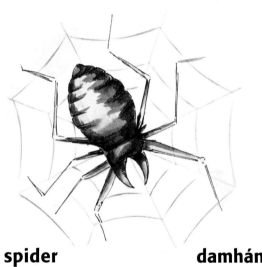

spider   **damhán alla**
daw-wawn olla

spiderweb   **líon damháin alla**
lee-un daw-wain olla

spoon   **spúnóg**
spoon-owg

squirrel   **iora rua**
ir-a roo-a

stairs **staighre**
sty-r'i

stamp **stampa**
stom-pa

starfish **crosóg mhara**
kruss-owg vor-a

stork **corr bhán**
kur vawn

stove **sornóg**
sowr-nog

strawberry **sú talún**
soo tol-oon

subway

fobhealach
fu-v'aluch

sugar cube

ciúb siúcra
k'oob shook-ra

sun

grian
g'r'ee-an

sunflower

lus na gréine
luss na gr'ayn'-i

sweater

geansaí
g'an-see

(to) sweep

scuab
skoo-ab

swing

luascán
loo-askawn

table   **bord**
bowrd

teapot   **taephota**
tay-futa

teddy bear   **béirín**
b'ayr'-een'

television   **teilifíseán**
t'el'-if'-eeshawn

10

ten   **deich**
d'eh

tent   **puball**
pub-ul

theater　　**amharclann**
owrk-lun

thimble　　**méaracán**
m'ayr-akawn

(to) think　　**smaoinigh**
smween'-ee

three　　**trí**
t'r'ee

tie　　**carbhat**
kor-avot

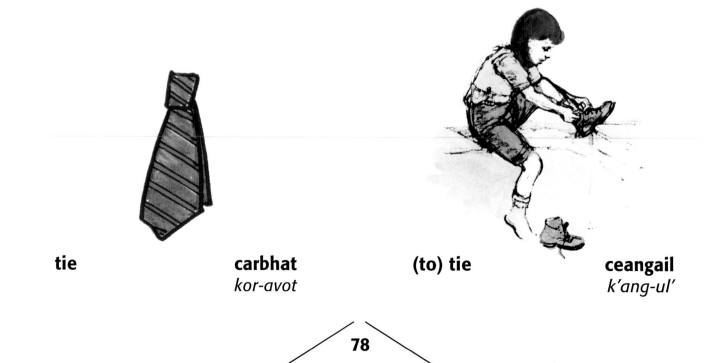

(to) tie　　**ceangail**
k'ang-ul'

tiger **tíogar**
t'eegur

toaster **tóastaer**
towss-tayr

tomato **tráta**
traw-ta

toucan **túcán**
too-kawn

towel **tuáille**
too-awl'i

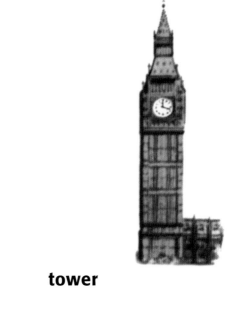

tower **túr**
toor

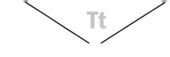

toy box　　**bosca bréagán**
buss-ka b'r'ay-gawn

tracks　　**ráillí**
raw-l'ee

train station　　**stáisiún traenach**
staw-shoon trayn-uch

tray　　**tráidire**
traw-d'ir'í

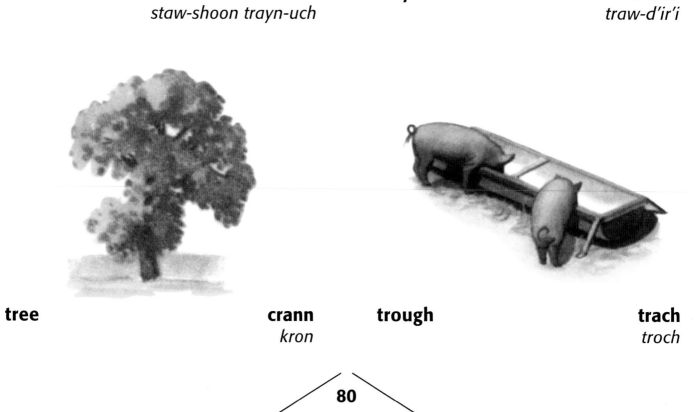

tree　　**crann**
kron

trough　　**trach**
troch

truck

trucail
truk-ul'

trumpet **troimpéad**
trum'-p'ayd

tulip

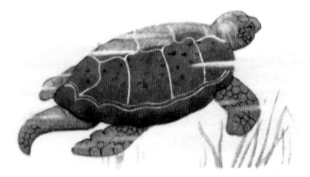

tiúilip
t'oo'-l'ip'

tunnel **tollán**
tul-awn

turtle **turtar**
tur-tur

twins **cúpla**
koop-la

two **dhá**
gaw

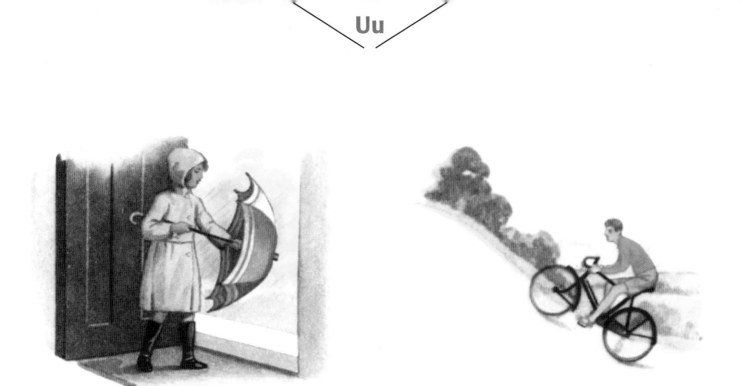

umbrella   **scáth fearthainne**   **uphill**   **i gcoinne an aird**
                   skaw f'ar-hin'i   *igun'-unawrd'*

vase   **vása**   **veil**   **fial**
               vaw-sa   *f'ee-al*

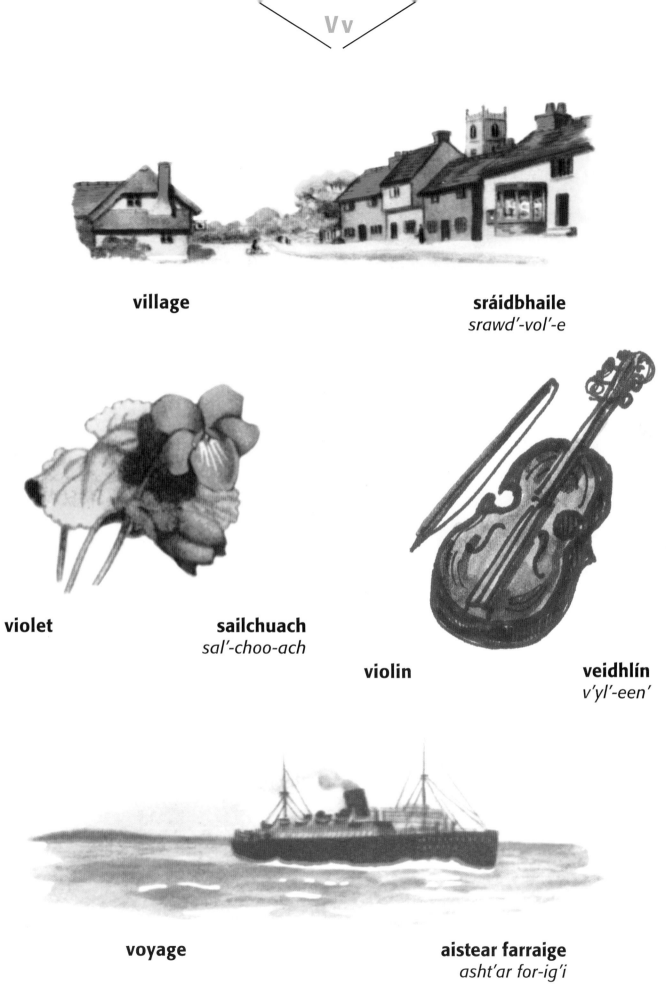

village

sráidbhaile
srawd'-vol'-e

violet

sailchuach
sal'-choo-ach

violin

veidhlín
v'yl'-een'

voyage

aistear farraige
asht'ar for-ig'i

waiter   **freastalaí**
frass-tulee

(to) wake up   **dúisigh**
doosh-ee

walrus   **rosualt**
rusoo-alt

(to) wash   **folc**
fulk

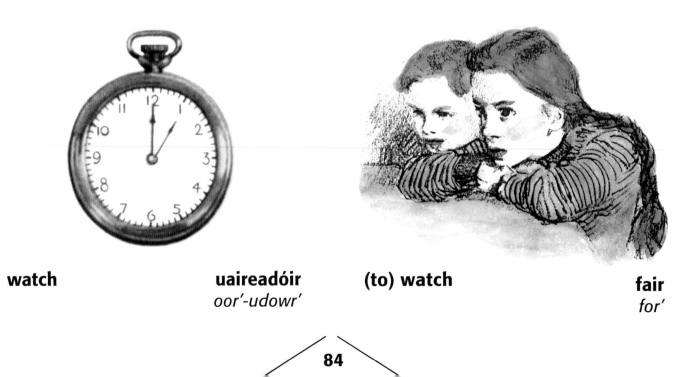

watch   **uaireadóir**
oor'-udowr'

(to) watch   **fair**
for'

(to) water   **uiscigh**
ish-k'ee

waterfall   **eas**
ass

watering can   **fraschanna**
fross-chon-a

watermelon   **mealbhacán**
m'al-avakawn

weather vane   **eite aimsire**
et'-i am'-shir'i

(to) weigh   **méaigh**
m'aw-ee

whale   **míol mór**
m'eel mowr

wheel   **roth**
ru

wheelbarrow   **barra rotha**
borra-a ru-hu

whiskers   **féasóg leicinn**
f'ays-owg l'ek'in'

(to) whisper   **siosc**
shisk

whistle   **fead**
f'ad

white **bán**
bawn

wig **bréagfholt**
br'ayg-ult

wind **gaoth**
gwee

window **fuinneog**
fin'-owg

wings **sciatháin**
shk'ee-ahawn'

winter **geimhreadh**
gev'-r'a

wolf

mac tíre
mok t'eer'-i

wood

adhmad
eye-mod

word

focal
fuk-ul

(to) write

scríobh
shk'r'eev

yellow

buí
bwee

Zz

zebra

séabra
sheeb-ra

A

abhainn	river
adhairt	pillow
adharca	horns
adhmad	wood
aghaidh	face
aibítir	alphabet
ailigéadar	Alligator
áilteor	clown
airgead	money
aistear farraige	voyage
amharclann	theater
ámóg	hammock
anann	pineapple
antalóp	antelope
aoibh	smile
aoire	shepherd
aon	one
aosta	old
ar oscailt	open
arán	bread
arbhar	corn
asal	donkey
athair	father

B

babaí	baby
babhla	bowl
bábóg	doll
bád	boat
bagáiste	luggage
báicéir	baker
bairéad	cap
bairille	barrel
báisteach	rain
balún	balloon
bán	white
banana	banana
banríon	queen
barra rotha	wheelbarrow
bascaed	basket
béabhar	beaver
beacán	mushroom

beach	bee
beag	small
béal	mouth
beanna	antlers
béar	bear
béar bán	polar bear
béar cóála	koala bear
béirín	teddy bear
binse	bench
biorán	pin
biorán sábháilteachta	safety pin
bláth	blossom; flower
bloic	blocks
bó	cow
bóin De	ladybug
bolgán solais	lightbulb
bord	table
bord faisnéise	bulletin board
bosca bréagán	toy box
bóthar	road
bráisléad	bracelet
bratach	flag
bréagfholt	wig
bricfeasta	breakfast
brioscóg	cracker
broc	badger
bróg	shoe
bronntanas	present
buachaill	boy
buatais	boot
buí	white
buicéad	bucket
buidéal	bottle
bumbóg	bumblebee

C

cab	cab
cabáiste	cabbage
cabhsa	path
cáca	cake
cachtas	cactus
caife	café
cailín	girl
cairéad	carrot
cairpéad	carpet
cáis	cheese

caisearbhán	dandelion
caisleán	castle
camall	camel
can	(to) sing
cangarú	kangaroo
caoin	(to) cry
caora	sheep
capall	horse
captaen	captain
cara	friend
carbhat	tie
carr	car
carr sleamhnáin	sled
cárta	card
casóg	jacket
casúr	hammer
cat	cat
cathaoir	chair
ceamara	camera
ceangail	(to) tie
ceannbheart	headdress
cearc	hen
ceathair	four
ceil	(to) hide
ceol	music
ciaróg	beetle
ciarsúr	handkerchief
cíor	comb
cith	shower
ciúb siúcra	sugar cube
ciúbanna oighir	ice cubes
cleite	feather
cliabhán	cradle
cling	(to) ring
clog	bell
clúdach litreach	envelope
cnámh	bone
cnapsac	backpack
cniotáil	(to) knit
cnó	nut
cnó cócó	coconut
cócaráil	(to) cook
codail	(to) sleep

coileach rooster
coileán puppy
coinín rabbit
coinneal candle
cóiste coach
colúr pigeon
comhla shutter
compás compass
corc cork
coróin crown
corr bhán stork
cos foot; leg
cóta coat
cóta báistí raincoat
cothaigh (to) feed
crann tree
crann giúise fir tree
crann Nollag Christmas tree
crann pailme palm tree
crann péine pine
craobh branch
criathar sieve
crios belt
cró madra doghouse
croí heart
crosóg mhara starfish
crú capaill horseshoe
cruinneog globe
cruinnigh (to) gather
crúsca pitcher
cuachadh (to) hug
cúcamar cucumber
cúig five
cuilteog leapa comforter
cuirtín curtain
cuisneoir refrigerator
cúpla twins

D

damh ox
damhán alla spider
damhsaigh (to) dance

dáta date
dathadóir painter
dathaigh paint
déanamh spraoi (to) play
dearg red
deartháir brother
deasc desk
deich ten
deilbh frame
deilf dolphin
déshúiligh binoculars
dhá two
díon roof
doirt (to) pour
donn brown
dorn fist
dornóg mitten
dragan dragon
draíodóir magician
dreap (to) climb
dréimire ladder
dreoilín teaspaigh grasshopper
droichead bridge
druma drum
dubh black
duileog leaf
duileog mailpe maple leaf
dúisigh (to) wake up

E

eagla fear
éan bird
éanadán birdcage
eas waterfall
eilifint elephant
eiscimeach Eskimo
éist (to) listen
eite aimsire weather vane
eitil (to) fly
eitleán airplane
eochair key
eorna barley

F

fáinne ring
fair (to) watch
fál fence
faoileán seagull
fásach desert
fead whistle
fean fan
fear bainne milkman
féar hay
féasóg leicinn whiskers
féileacán butterfly
feileastram iris
fia deer
fial veil
filiméala nightingale
fíonchaora grapes
fobhealach subway
focal word
folamh empty
folc (to) wash
fómhar autumn
fómhar harvest
forc fork
fraschanna watering can
fréamh root
freastalaí waiter
frog frog
fuaigh (to) sew
fuarán fountain
fuinneog window

G

gabhar goat
gairdín garden
gáire laughter
gaoth wind
gé goose
gealach moon
gealbhan sparrow
geansaí sweater

geata gate
geimhreadh winter
geiréiniam geranium
giotár guitar
glas lock
glas crochta padlock
gléas instrument
gliomach lobster
gloine glass
gorm blue
gráinneog hedgehog
grian sun
gúna dress

H

hamstar hamster
hata hat
hiodrant hydrant

I

i gcoinne an aird uphill
ialtóg bat
iarann iron
iasc fish
iasc órga goldfish
iascach (to) fish
inneall engine
iolar eagle
iompair (to) carry
iora rua squirrel
iris magazine
ith (to) eat

J

jacaí jockey

L

labhandar lavender
lacha duck
lámh hand
lámhacán (to) crawl
lámhainn glove
lámhchleasaí juggler
lampa lamp

leaba bed
leabhar nótaí notebook
leabhar book
léarscáil map
léigh (to) read
léim (to) jump
léine shirt
leitis lettuce
leon lion
liathchorcra lilac
liathróid ball
lincse lynx
linéar aigéin ocean liner
línigh (to) draw
liomóid lemon
lión damháin alla spiderweb
logall pit
lomaire faiche lawn mower
lománaí lumberjack
lón lunch
long ship
luascán swing
luch fhéir field mouse
luch(óg) mouse
lus na gréine sunflower

M

mac tíre wolf
madra dog
maide corrach seesaw
maighnéad magnet
mairnéalach sailor
mála láimhe handbag
margadh marketplace
masc mask
máthair mother
meáigh (to) weigh
mealbhacán watermelon
méar finger
méaracán thimble
mil honey
milseán candy
míol mór whale
míreanna mearaí jigsaw puzzle
moncaí monkey

mórbhealach highway
muc pig
muince necklace

N

naoi nine
naomhóg canoe
nathair snake
nead nest
néal cloud
nocht naked
nuachtán newspaper

O

ocht eight
oíche mhaith "Good night"
oighearscátáil ice-skating
oileán island
oinniún onion
ól (to) drink; (to) lap
oráiste orange
orláiste hourglass
ostrais ostrich

P

páipéar paper
páirc field
páirc park
paiste patch
parasiút parachute
pas passport
peann luaidhe pencil

S

pearaicít	lovebird
pearóid	parrot
peileacán	pelican
péitseog	peach
pianó	piano
picil	pickle
pioc	(to) peck
pióg	pie
piongain	penguin
piorra	pear
piscín	kitten
pitseámaí	pajamas
pláta	plate
platapas	platypus
pluais	cave
pluma	plum
pobal	people
pónaí	pony
pota	pot
práta	potato
puball	tent
puimcín	pumpkin
púróg	pebble

R

racún	raccoon
rafta	raft
raicéad	racket
raidió	radio
raidis	radish
ráillí	tracks
raithneach	fern
rámh	oar
rámhaigh	(to) row
rialóir	ruler
ridire	knight
rith	(to) run
roicéad	rocket
rópa	rope
rós	rose
rosualt	walrus
roth	heel
rothar	bicycle

saighead	arrow
sailchuach	violet
salach	dirty
salann	salt
scaif	scarf
scamh	(to) peel
scáth fearthainne	umbrella
scáthán	mirror
scian	knife
sciatháin	wings
scoil	school
scríobh	(to) write
scriúire	screwdriver
scuabadh	(to) sweep
scuab	broom; brush
sé	six
séabra	zebra
seacht	seven
seacláid	chocolate
seanathair	grandfather
seanmháthair	grandmother
seol	(to) sail
silide	snail
silín	cherry
simléar	chimney
sionnach	fox
sioráf	giraffe
siorc	shark
siosc	(to) whisper
siosúr	scissors
slán	"Good-bye"
sliabh	mountain
sliogán	shell
sluasaid	shovel
smaoinigh	(to) think

snaidhm	knot
snámh	(to) float
snáthaid mhór	dragonfly
snáthaid	needle
sneachta	snow
sorcas	circus
sornóg	stove
spéaclaí	glasses
splancsolas	flashlight
spúnóg	spoon
sráidbhaile	village
sraimlí	messy
srónbheannach	rhinoceros
staighre beo	escalator
staighre	stairs
stáisiún traenach	train station
stampa	stamp
stoca	sock
stua	arch
sú craobh	raspberry
sú talún	strawberry
subh	jam
suigh	(to) sit
súil	eye

T

tabhair	(to) give
taephota	teapot
taiscéal	(to) explore
taispéain	(to) show
tarraing	(to) pull
teach	house
teach bábóg	dollhouse
teach gloine	greenhouse
teach solais	lighthouse
teilifíseán	television
tine	fire
tinn	sick
tíogar	tiger
tiúilip	tulip
tóastaer	toaster
tolg	sofa
tollán	tunnel

Folk Tales from Bohemia
Adolf Wenig
This folk tale collection is one of a kind, focusing uniquely on humankind's struggle with evil in the world. Delicately ornate red and black text and illustrations set the mood.
Ages 9 and up
90 pages • red and black illustrations • 5 1/2 x 8 1/4 • 0-7818-0718-2 • W • $14.95hc • (786)

Czech, Moravian and Slovak Fairy Tales
Parker Fillmore
Fifteen different classic, regional folk tales and 23 charming illustrations whisk the reader to places of romance, deception, royalty, and magic.
Ages 12 and up
243 pages • 23 b/w illustrations • 5 1/2 x 8 1/4 • 0-7818-0714-X • W • $14.95 hc • (792)

Glass Mountain: Twenty-Eight Ancient Polish Folk Tales and Fables
W.S. Kuniczak
Illustrated by Pat Bargielski
As a child in a far-away misty corner of Volhynia, W.S. Kuniczak was carried away to an extraordinary world of magic and illusion by the folk tales of his Polish nurse.
171 pages • 6 x 9 • 8 illustrations • 0-7818-0552-X • W • $16.95hc • (645)

Old Polish Legends
Retold by F.C. Anstruther
Wood engravings by J. Sekalski
This fine collection of eleven fairy tales, with an introduction by Zymunt Nowakowski, was first published in Scotland during World War II.
66 pages • 7 1/4 x 9 • 11 woodcut engravings • 0-7818-0521-X • W • $11.95hc • (653)

Folk Tales from Russia
by Donald A. Mackenzie
With nearly 200 pages and 8 full-page black-and-white illustrations, the reader will be charmed by these legendary folk tales that symbolically weave magical fantasy with the historic events of Russia's past.
Ages 12 and up
192 pages • 8 b/w illustrations • 5 1/2 x 8 1/4 • 0-7818-0696-8 • W • $12.50hc • (**788**)

Fairy Gold: A Book of Classic English Fairy Tales
Chosen by Ernest Rhys
Illustrated by Herbert Cole
Forty-nine imaginative black and white illustrations accompany thirty classic tales, including such beloved stories as "Jack and the Bean Stalk" and "The Three Bears."
Ages 12 and up
236 pages • 5 1/2 x 8 1/4 • 49 b/w illustrations • 0-7818-0700-X • W • $14.95hc • (790)

Tales of Languedoc: From the South of France

Samuel Jacques Brun

For readers of all ages, here is a masterful collection of folk tales from the south of France.

Ages 12 and up

248 pages • 33 b/w sketches • 5 1/2 x 8 1/4 • 0-7818-0715-8 • W • $14.95hc • (793)

Twenty Scottish Tales and Legends

Edited by Cyril Swinson

Illustrated by Allan Stewart

Twenty enchanting stories take the reader to an extraordinary world of magic harps, angry giants, mysterious spells and gallant Knights.

Ages 9 and up

215 pages • 5 1/2 x 8 1/4 • 8 b/w illustrations • 0-7818-0701-8 • W • $14.95 hc • (789)

Swedish Fairy Tales

Translated by H. L. Braekstad

A unique blending of enchantment, adventure, comedy, and romance make this collection of Swedish fairy tales a must-have for any library.

Ages 9 and up

190 pages • 21 b/w illustrations • 51/2 x 81/4 • 0-7818-0717-4 • W • $12.50hc • (787)

The Little Mermaid and Other Tales

Hans Christian Andersen

Here is a near replica of the first American edition of 27 classic fairy tales from the masterful Hans Christian Andersen.

Ages 9 and up

508 pages • b/w illustrations • 6 x 9 • 0-7818-0720-4 • W • $19.95hc • (791)

Pakistani Folk Tales: Toontoony Pie and Other Stories

Ashraf Siddiqui and Marilyn Lerch

Illustrated by Jan Fairservis

In these 22 folk tales are found not only the familiar figures of folklore—kings and beautiful princesses—but the magic of the Far East, cunning jackals, and wise holy men.

Ages 7 and up

158 pages • 6 1/2 x 8 1/2 • 38 illustrations • 0-7818-0703-4 • W • $12.50hc • (784)

Folk Tales from Chile

Brenda Hughes

This selection of 15 tales gives a taste of the variety of Chile's rich folklore. Fifteen charming illustrations accompany the text.

Ages 7 and up

121 pages • 5 1/2 x 8 1/4 • 15 illustrations • 0-7818-0712-3 • W • $12.50hc • (785)

All prices subject to change. **To purchase Hippocrene Books** contact your local bookstore, call (718) 454-2366, or write to: HIPPOCRENE BOOKS, 171 Madison Avenue, New York, NY 10016. Please enclose check or money order, adding $5.00 shipping (UPS) for the first book and $.50 for each additional book.